CHECKERBOARD BIOGRAPHY LIBRARY

U.S. PRESIDENTS

The
United States Presidents

DWIGHT D. EISENHOWER

ABDO Publishing Company

Tamara L. Britton

visit us at
www.abdopublishing.com

Printed in the United States of America, North Mankato, Minnesota.
012009 082013

Cover Photo: Getty Images
Interior Photos: AP Images pp. 9, 10, 16, 17, 19, 26, 27; Corbis pp. 5, 11, 12, 13, 25;
    Getty Images pp. 15, 18, 20, 23, 29; iStockphoto p. 32

Editor: Megan M. Gunderson
Art Direction & Cover Design: Neil Klinepier
Interior Design: Jaime Martens

Library of Congress Cataloging-in-Publication Data

Britton, Tamara L., 1963-
  Dwight D. Eisenhower / Tamara L. Britton.
    p. cm. -- (The United States presidents)
  Includes bibliographical references and index.
  ISBN 978-1-60453-449-8
  1. Eisenhower, Dwight D. (Dwight David), 1890-1969--Juvenile literature. 2. Presidents--United
States--Biography--Juvenile literature. I. Title.

  E836.B748 2009
  973.921092--dc22
  [B]
                                        2008040976

CONTENTS

DWIGHT D. EISENHOWER

General Dwight D. Eisenhower was one of the most successful military leaders in U.S. history. He commanded the **Allies** in Europe during **World War II**. When the war ended, Eisenhower continued on in the military as the army **chief of staff**. Later, he became the first head of **NATO** forces.

In 1952, Eisenhower easily defeated Adlai E. Stevenson II in the presidential election. Eisenhower took office in January 1953. He was the first **Republican** president in 20 years.

Under Eisenhower's leadership, businesses did well. Most Americans had jobs. And, Eisenhower met with world leaders to make peace.

Americans liked President Eisenhower and the way he ran the country. He had an easygoing personality and a cheerful grin. He was an honorable man.

TIMELINE

1890 - Dwight David Eisenhower was born on October 14 in Denison, Texas.

1915 - Eisenhower graduated from the U.S. Military Academy at West Point in New York.

1916 - On July 1, Eisenhower married Mary "Mamie" Doud.

1933 - Eisenhower became General Douglas MacArthur's assistant.

1941 - The United States entered World War II.

1942 - Eisenhower was transferred to London, England, to command U.S. forces in Europe; Eisenhower was in charge of the invasion of North Africa.

1943 - Eisenhower was named supreme commander of the Allied Expeditionary Force in Europe.

1944 - Operation Overlord began on June 6; Eisenhower was named a five-star general on December 20.

1945 - The war ended in Europe on May 8; Eisenhower was named army chief of staff.

1948 - Eisenhower retired from the army; Eisenhower became president of Columbia University.

1953 - On January 20, Eisenhower became the thirty-fourth president.

1956 - Eisenhower was reelected U.S. president.

1957 - Congress approved the Eisenhower Doctrine; Eisenhower sent the U.S. Army's 101st Airborne unit to Little Rock Central High School in Little Rock, Arkansas; Eisenhower signed the Civil Rights Act of 1957; the Soviets launched *Sputnik I*.

1969 - Dwight D. Eisenhower died on March 28.

DID YOU KNOW?

President Dwight D. Eisenhower believed that new, multilane highways would aid in national defense. On June 29, 1956, he signed the Federal Aid Highway Act. It created the Eisenhower Interstate Highway system.

President Franklin D. Roosevelt built a presidential retreat in Maryland. He named it Shangri-La. President Eisenhower later renamed the retreat Camp David after his grandson.

Alaska officially became the forty-ninth state on January 3, 1959. On August 21, 1959, Hawaii became the fiftieth state. President Eisenhower was the first president to govern all 50 United States.

Eisenhower's given name was David Dwight Eisenhower. However, he was called Dwight so he wouldn't be confused with his father. Later in life, Eisenhower officially changed his name to Dwight David.

YOUNG DWIGHT

Dwight David Eisenhower was born on October 14, 1890, in Denison, Texas. His parents were David and Ida Eisenhower. The Eisenhowers raised six sons. They were Dwight, Arthur, Edgar, Roy, Earl, and Milton.

The Eisenhowers moved to Abilene, Kansas, when Dwight was two years old. They lived in a house his grandfather had built. Dwight's friends called him Ike. The nickname stayed with him his whole life.

Ike was a good student. He did well in English, history, and geometry. He was a friendly person and a good athlete. In high school, Ike played both basketball and football.

Ike graduated from Abilene High School in 1909. For the next two years, he worked to help his family. The money Ike made allowed his brother Edgar to attend college.

FAST FACTS

BORN - October 14, 1890

WIFE - Mary "Mamie" Doud (1896–1979)

CHILDREN - 2

POLITICAL PARTY - Republican

AGE AT INAUGURATION - 62

YEARS SERVED - 1953–1961

VICE PRESIDENT - Richard Nixon

DIED - March 28, 1969, age 78

Dwight (far left) *with his family*

Since his family didn't have much money, Ike decided to attend military school. In 1911, he entered the U.S. Military Academy at West Point in New York. There, his education would be free. And, he could play on the academy's football team.

COLLEGE AND MARRIAGE

Eisenhower loved playing football at West Point. He was an excellent player. But, he hurt his knee during his second year. The injury ended his football career forever. It was a crushing blow. Eisenhower had trouble adjusting to life without football.

In college, Eisenhower was an average student. His **rebellious** nature earned him many **demerits**. Still, he graduated from West Point in 1915. Eisenhower was sixty-first in his class of 164 students.

After graduation, Eisenhower became a second lieutenant in the U.S. Army. Two weeks later, he reported for duty. His first military assignment was at Fort Sam Houston in Texas.

On a weekend off, Eisenhower went to nearby San Antonio. There, he met Mary "Mamie" Doud. On July 1, 1916, the two

Ike and Mamie in 1918, soon after their marriage

married. That same day, Eisenhower was promoted to first lieutenant.

In 1917, the Eisenhowers welcomed their first child. They named him Doud but called him Icky. When he was only three years old, Icky became ill and died. For the rest of his life, Eisenhower sent his wife flowers on Icky's birthday.

The Eisenhowers with their son Doud

MILITARY MAN

Eisenhower was promoted to captain in 1917. He was eager to go to Europe to fight in **World War I**. But army officials believed he could better serve by training new soldiers. So in 1918, Eisenhower was named head of Camp Colt. This was a training base in Gettysburg, Pennsylvania. For his efforts, Eisenhower was promoted to major in 1920. He also received the Distinguished Service Medal.

In 1922, Eisenhower was transferred to the **Panama Canal Zone**. He went to protect the new canal. Mrs. Eisenhower

MacArthur (left) *and Eisenhower*

disliked the uncivilized conditions in Panama. So, she often stayed in Denver, Colorado, with her family. There, the Eisenhowers welcomed a second son they named John.

The Panama Canal opened on August 15, 1914.

To advance his career, Eisenhower attended the Command and General Staff School in Leavenworth, Kansas. There, he was a hardworking student. This time, he graduated first in his class of 275 students.

The army recognized Eisenhower as an outstanding officer. In 1933, he became General Douglas MacArthur's assistant. Eisenhower helped MacArthur develop a defense plan in the Philippines.

Eisenhower had a successful career in the army. But he was unsatisfied. Eisenhower wanted to command troops. **World War II** soon provided him this opportunity.

WORLD WAR II

In 1941, the United States entered **World War II**. Eisenhower was promoted to colonel and then brigadier general. The next year, he moved up to major general and then lieutenant general. In 1942, his hard work paid off. He was transferred to London, England, to command U.S. forces in Europe.

General Eisenhower was in charge of the invasion of North Africa in July 1942. American forces planned to move east to meet British forces that were moving west from Egypt.

Eisenhower's men met early defeats. Then, Eisenhower put General George Patton in charge. After seven months, the Americans met up with the British and defeated the Germans. This victory earned Eisenhower a promotion to four-star general.

Army officials recognized Eisenhower's talent for getting different groups to cooperate and reach a common goal. So in 1943, Eisenhower was named supreme commander of the **Allied** Expeditionary Force in Europe. In this role, he would carry out Operation Overlord. This was the code name for an invasion of Western Europe.

Allied forces meet in North Africa

On June 6, 1944, the **Allies** landed in Normandy, France. This is known as D-day. In six days the beach was secure. The Germans fled east across Europe. On August 25, the Allies freed Paris, France, from German control. Then, the Allies forced the Germans all the way back to Germany.

Operation Overlord was one of the greatest operations in military history. Because of its success, Eisenhower was named a five-star general on December 20, 1944.

General Eisenhower instructed the troops on the day before D-day.

While **Allied** forces attacked Germany from the west, the Russians advanced from the east. On May 1, 1945, the Russians captured Berlin, Germany. Seven days later, the Germans surrendered. The war in Europe was over. Later that year, Eisenhower was named army **chief of staff**.

In 1948, he retired from the army. That same year, Eisenhower became the president of Columbia University in New York City, New York. He also wrote a best-selling book about his **World War II** experience. The book is titled *Crusade in Europe*.

Five-star general is the nation's highest military rank.

A STRONG LEADER

In 1950, President Harry S. Truman requested Eisenhower's help in starting **NATO**. Eisenhower was named supreme commander of NATO's forces.

The document signed by NATO members appointing Eisenhower supreme commander

Americans saw Eisenhower as a great leader. They believed he would make an able president. Both **Democrats** and **Republicans** approached him about running for president. Eisenhower was honored.

Eisenhower chose to run as a Republican. On June 4, 1952, he gave a speech in his hometown of Abilene, Kansas. With this, Eisenhower officially entered the presidential race.

During this time, the United States was fighting the **Korean War**. While campaigning, Eisenhower assured Americans that he would work for world peace. To end the Korean War, he promised, "I shall go to Korea."

Republicans chose Eisenhower as their candidate for president. California senator Richard Nixon became his **running mate**. Eisenhower's **Democratic** challenger was Illinois governor Adlai E. Stevenson II. Stevenson's running mate was Senator John Sparkman of Alabama.

As supreme commander, Eisenhower worked at NATO headquarters in Paris, France.

PRESIDENT EISENHOWER

On November 4, 1952, Eisenhower was elected the thirty-fourth president of the United States. He received nearly 34 million votes. It was the most ever won by a presidential candidate at that time.

Eisenhower was **inaugurated** on January 20, 1953. Four weeks later, President Eisenhower kept his campaign promise. He went to Korea. President Eisenhower visited the battlefields and worked for a peaceful settlement to the conflict. On July 27, 1953, a peace agreement ended the **Korean War**.

President Eisenhower reviewed South Korean troops during his visit.

PRESIDENT EISENHOWER'S CABINET

FIRST TERM
JANUARY 20, 1953–
JANUARY 20, 1957

- **STATE –** John Foster Dulles
- **TREASURY –** George M. Humphrey
- **DEFENSE –** Charles E. Wilson
- **ATTORNEY GENERAL –** Herbert Brownell Jr.
- **INTERIOR –** Douglas McKay
  Frederick A. Seaton (from June 8, 1956)
- **AGRICULTURE –** Ezra Taft Benson
- **COMMERCE –** Sinclair Weeks
- **LABOR –** Martin P. Durkin
  James P. Mitchell (from October 9, 1953)
- **HEALTH, EDUCATION, AND WELFARE –**
  Oveta Culp Hobby (from April 11, 1953)
  Marion B. Folsom (from August 1, 1955)

SECOND TERM
JANUARY 20, 1957–
JANUARY 20, 1961

- **STATE –** John Foster Dulles
  Christian A. Herter (from April 22, 1959)
- **TREASURY –** George M. Humphrey
  Robert B. Anderson (from July 29, 1957)
- **DEFENSE –** Charles E. Wilson
  Neil H. McElroy (from October 9, 1957)
  Thomas S. Gates Jr. (from December 2, 1959)
- **ATTORNEY GENERAL –** Herbert Brownell Jr.
  William P. Rogers (from January 27, 1958)
- **INTERIOR –** Frederick A. Seaton
- **AGRICULTURE –** Ezra Taft Benson
- **COMMERCE –** Sinclair Weeks
  Frederick H. Mueller (from August 10, 1959)
- **LABOR –** James P. Mitchell
- **HEALTH, EDUCATION, AND WELFARE –**
  Marion B. Folsom
  Arthur S. Flemming (from August 1, 1958)

On May 17, 1954, the U.S. **Supreme Court** ruled on the case of *Brown v. Board of Education of Topeka*. It said that separating children of different races in public schools was **unconstitutional**. Schools across the nation were to be **integrated** immediately.

Another important event happened on April 12, 1955. Doctor Jonas E. Salk of Pittsburgh, Pennsylvania, discovered a drug to stop **polio**. Millions of people had suffered from this disease.

President Eisenhower worked with Secretary of Health and Human Services Oveta Hobby. Together, they came up with a plan to give the drug to Americans. Today, polio has almost been erased in the United States.

On September 24, 1955, President Eisenhower and the whole country suffered a scare. While on vacation in Colorado, he had a heart attack. It was a few months before the president fully recovered.

In December, President Eisenhower was ready to return to work. Many Americans wondered if he would run for a second term. Eisenhower told the nation he would run for reelection.

SUPREME COURT APPOINTMENTS

EARL WARREN - 1953
JOHN MARSHALL HARLAN - 1955
WILLIAM J. BRENNAN JR. - 1956
CHARLES WHITTAKER - 1957
POTTER STEWART - 1958

Oveta Hobby (above) *was only the second woman to serve on a president's cabinet. The first was Frances Perkins, President Franklin D. Roosevelt's secretary of labor.*

A SECOND TERM

In 1956, the **Democrats** again chose Adlai E. Stevenson II as their presidential candidate. In this election, his **running mate** was Senator Estes Kefauver of Tennessee. President Eisenhower and Vice President Nixon ran on the **Republican** ticket.

In November, Eisenhower and Nixon were easily reelected. But Eisenhower faced problems both at home and abroad. In 1954, President Eisenhower had signed the Communist Control Act. This made the Communist Party in the United States unlawful.

But, people in other parts of the world were worried about the spread of Communism. President Eisenhower asked Congress for money to help any Middle Eastern nation that wanted to fight its spread. Congress approved this plan in March 1957. It became known as the Eisenhower Doctrine.

At home, it was a difficult time in American history. **Riots** and peaceful protests were going on throughout the country. African Americans and their supporters were fighting for **civil rights**.

In the South, many people wanted separate schools for white and black children. They also wanted separate water fountains and restaurants. African Americans were forced to sit in the back of buses. And, laws were passed to keep them from voting.

There was also resistance to the *Brown v. Board of Education of Topeka* ruling. In September 1957, nine African-American students were enrolled at Little Rock Central High School in Little Rock, Arkansas. Mobs of white people tried to keep the children from entering the school building. Governor Orval Faubus sent the Arkansas **National Guard** to keep the students out of school.

Elizabeth Eckford was one of the nine African-American students enrolled in Central High School. She had to walk to class amid taunts from white students.

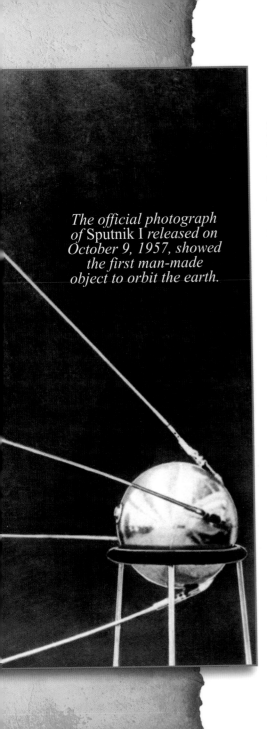

The official photograph of Sputnik I *released on October 9, 1957, showed the first man-made object to orbit the earth.*

As president, Eisenhower's job was to protect and defend the U.S. **Constitution**. He sent the U.S. Army's 101st Airborne unit to protect the children's constitutional rights. The soldiers made sure the children were allowed into the school. The children had military protection for the entire school year.

That same year, Eisenhower signed the **Civil Rights** Act of 1957. The law secured the voting rights of African Americans. It ended legal **segregation**. It also created the Civil Rights Commission.

That same year, the Soviet Union put the first **satellite** into space. They launched *Sputnik I* on October 4, 1957. So in 1958, President Eisenhower asked Congress to create a space agency. The organization would research and explore the universe. Congress approved Eisenhower's plan. The National Aeronautics and Space Administration (NASA) was formed.

Government officials were concerned about Soviet intentions. They wanted to see if the Soviets had more **missiles** than the United States. So, air force pilots flew spy airplanes over the Soviet Union.

On May 1, 1960, the Soviets shot down one of the spy airplanes. They captured its pilot, Francis Gary Powers. Eisenhower then had to admit the United States was spying.

As a result, Soviet leader Nikita Khrushchev refused to attend a meeting to discuss reducing weapons production. President Eisenhower was disappointed.

Khrushchev (left) visited Eisenhower in the United States in 1959. The spy airplane incident obstructed Eisenhower's efforts to improve relations between the two nations.

He had seen the horrors of war. He regretted that he could not do more to protect future generations from its effects.

HOME AT LAST

On February 27, 1951, a new **amendment** had been added to the U.S. **Constitution**. The Twenty-second Amendment said that no one could be president more than two terms. Eisenhower was the first president required by this new law to leave the White House.

January 20, 1961, was Eisenhower's last day as president. That day, John F. Kennedy took office. He had defeated Vice President Richard Nixon to become the new president.

Eisenhower retired to his farm in Gettysburg, Pennsylvania. He raised animals and played golf. He also spent time with his family and wrote his **memoirs**.

Throughout 1968, Eisenhower's health worsened. He was in the hospital for almost a year. Then on March 28, 1969, Dwight D. Eisenhower died of heart failure.

Eisenhower was buried in Abilene, Kansas, in the chapel at the Eisenhower Center. The military hero and president was honored with a three-day funeral service. It drew world leaders and everyday citizens who loved and respected him.

President Eisenhower's funeral was held at the Eisenhower Center in Abilene, Kansas.

At the time of Eisenhower's death, former vice president Richard Nixon was president. At Eisenhower's funeral, Nixon revealed some of Eisenhower's last words. Eisenhower had said, "I've always loved my wife. I've always loved my children. I've always loved my grandchildren. I've always loved my country."

OFFICE OF THE PRESIDENT

BRANCHES OF GOVERNMENT

The U.S. government is divided into three branches. They are the executive, legislative, and judicial branches. This division is called a separation of powers. Each branch has some power over the others. This is called a system of checks and balances.

EXECUTIVE BRANCH

The executive branch enforces laws. It is made up of the president, the vice president, and the president's cabinet. The president represents the United States around the world. He or she oversees relations with other countries and signs treaties. The president signs bills into law and appoints officials and federal judges. He or she also leads the military and manages government workers.

LEGISLATIVE BRANCH

The legislative branch makes laws, maintains the military, and regulates trade. It also has the power to declare war. This branch consists of the Senate and the House of Representatives. Together, these two houses make up Congress. Each state has two senators. A state's population determines the number of representatives it has.

JUDICIAL BRANCH

The judicial branch interprets laws. It consists of district courts, courts of appeals, and the Supreme Court. District courts try cases. If a person disagrees with a trial's outcome, he or she may appeal. If the courts of appeals support the ruling, a person may appeal to the Supreme Court. The Supreme Court also makes sure that laws follow the U.S. Constitution.

QUALIFICATIONS FOR OFFICE

To be president, a person must meet three requirements. A candidate must be at least 35 years old and a natural-born U.S. citizen. He or she must also have lived in the United States for at least 14 years.

ELECTORAL COLLEGE

The U.S. presidential election is an indirect election. Voters from each state choose electors to represent them in the Electoral College. The number of electors from each state is based on population. Each elector has one electoral vote. Electors are pledged to cast their vote for the candidate who receives the highest number of popular votes in their state. A candidate must receive the majority of Electoral College votes to win.

TERM OF OFFICE

Each president may be elected to two four-year terms. Sometimes, a president may only be elected once. This happens if he or she served more than two years of the previous president's term.

The presidential election is held on the Tuesday after the first Monday in November. The president is sworn in on January 20 of the following year. At that time, he or she takes the oath of office:

I do solemnly swear (or affirm) that I will faithfully execute the office of President of the United States, and will to the best of my ability, preserve, protect and defend the Constitution of the United States.

LINE OF SUCCESSION

The Presidential Succession Act of 1947 defines who becomes president if the president cannot serve. The vice president is first in the line of succession. Next are the Speaker of the House and the President Pro Tempore of the Senate. If none of these individuals is able to serve, the office falls to the president's cabinet members. They would take office in the order in which each department was created:

Secretary of State

Secretary of the Treasury

Secretary of Defense

Attorney General

Secretary of the Interior

Secretary of Agriculture

Secretary of Commerce

Secretary of Labor

Secretary of Health and Human Services

Secretary of Housing and Urban Development

Secretary of Transportation

Secretary of Energy

Secretary of Education

Secretary of Veterans Affairs

Secretary of Homeland Security

Benefits

• While in office, the president receives a salary of $400,000 each year. He or she lives in the White House and has 24-hour Secret Service protection.

• The president may travel on a Boeing 747 jet called Air Force One. The airplane can accommodate 70 passengers. It has kitchens, a dining room, sleeping areas, and a conference room. It also has fully equipped offices with the latest communications systems. Air Force One can fly halfway around the world before needing to refuel. It can even refuel in flight!

• If the president wishes to travel by car, he or she uses Cadillac One. Cadillac One is a Cadillac Deville. It has been modified with heavy armor and communications systems. The president takes Cadillac One along when visiting other countries if secure transportation will be needed.

• The president also travels on a helicopter called Marine One. Like the presidential car, Marine One accompanies the president when traveling abroad if necessary.

• Sometimes, the president needs to get away and relax with family and friends. Camp David is the official presidential retreat. It is located in the cool, wooded mountains in Maryland. The U.S. Navy maintains the retreat, and the U.S. Marine Corps keeps it secure. The camp offers swimming, tennis, golf, and hiking.

• When the president leaves office, he or she receives Secret Service protection for ten more years. He or she also receives a yearly pension of $191,300 and funding for office space, supplies, and staff.

PRESIDENTS AND THEIR TERMS

PRESIDENT	PARTY	TOOK OFFICE	LEFT OFFICE	TERMS SERVED	VICE PRESIDENT
George Washington	None	April 30, 1789	March 4, 1797	Two	John Adams
John Adams	Federalist	March 4, 1797	March 4, 1801	One	Thomas Jefferson
Thomas Jefferson	Democratic-Republican	March 4, 1801	March 4, 1809	Two	Aaron Burr, George Clinton
James Madison	Democratic-Republican	March 4, 1809	March 4, 1817	Two	George Clinton, Elbridge Gerry
James Monroe	Democratic-Republican	March 4, 1817	March 4, 1825	Two	Daniel D. Tompkins
John Quincy Adams	Democratic-Republican	March 4, 1825	March 4, 1829	One	John C. Calhoun
Andrew Jackson	Democrat	March 4, 1829	March 4, 1837	Two	John C. Calhoun, Martin Van Buren
Martin Van Buren	Democrat	March 4, 1837	March 4, 1841	One	Richard M. Johnson
William H. Harrison	Whig	March 4, 1841	April 4, 1841	Died During First Term	John Tyler
John Tyler	Whig	April 6, 1841	March 4, 1845	Completed Harrison's Term	Office Vacant
James K. Polk	Democrat	March 4, 1845	March 4, 1849	One	George M. Dallas
Zachary Taylor	Whig	March 5, 1849	July 9, 1850	Died During First Term	Millard Fillmore

PRESIDENT	PARTY	TOOK OFFICE	LEFT OFFICE	TERMS SERVED	VICE PRESIDENT
Millard Fillmore	Whig	July 10, 1850	March 4, 1853	Completed Taylor's Term	Office Vacant
Franklin Pierce	Democrat	March 4, 1853	March 4, 1857	One	William R.D. King
James Buchanan	Democrat	March 4, 1857	March 4, 1861	One	John C. Breckinridge
Abraham Lincoln	Republican	March 4, 1861	April 15, 1865	Served One Term, Died During Second Term	Hannibal Hamlin, Andrew Johnson
Andrew Johnson	Democrat	April 15, 1865	March 4, 1869	Completed Lincoln's Second Term	Office Vacant
Ulysses S. Grant	Republican	March 4, 1869	March 4, 1877	Two	Schuyler Colfax, Henry Wilson
Rutherford B. Hayes	Republican	March 3, 1877	March 4, 1881	One	William A. Wheeler
James A. Garfield	Republican	March 4, 1881	September 19, 1881	Died During First Term	Chester Arthur
Chester Arthur	Republican	September 20, 1881	March 4, 1885	Completed Garfield's Term	Office Vacant
Grover Cleveland	Democrat	March 4, 1885	March 4, 1889	One	Thomas A. Hendricks
Benjamin Harrison	Republican	March 4, 1889	March 4, 1893	One	Levi P. Morton
Grover Cleveland	Democrat	March 4, 1893	March 4, 1897	One	Adlai E. Stevenson
William McKinley	Republican	March 4, 1897	September 14, 1901	Served One Term, Died During Second Term	Garret A. Hobart, Theodore Roosevelt

PRESIDENTS 13–25, 1850–1901

PRESIDENT	PARTY	TOOK OFFICE	LEFT OFFICE	TERMS SERVED	VICE PRESIDENT
Theodore Roosevelt	Republican	September 14, 1901	March 4, 1909	Completed McKinley's Second Term, Served One Term	Office Vacant, Charles Fairbanks
William Taft	Republican	March 4, 1909	March 4, 1913	One	James S. Sherman
Woodrow Wilson	Democrat	March 4, 1913	March 4, 1921	Two	Thomas R. Marshall
Warren G. Harding	Republican	March 4, 1921	August 2, 1923	Died During First Term	Calvin Coolidge
Calvin Coolidge	Republican	August 3, 1923	March 4, 1929	Completed Harding's Term, Served One Term	Office Vacant, Charles Dawes
Herbert Hoover	Republican	March 4, 1929	March 4, 1933	One	Charles Curtis
Franklin D. Roosevelt	Democrat	March 4, 1933	April 12, 1945	Served Three Terms, Died During Fourth Term	John Nance Garner, Henry A. Wallace, Harry S. Truman
Harry S. Truman	Democrat	April 12, 1945	January 20, 1953	Completed Roosevelt's Fourth Term, Served One Term	Office Vacant, Alben Barkley
Dwight D. Eisenhower	Republican	January 20, 1953	January 20, 1961	Two	Richard Nixon
John F. Kennedy	Democrat	January 20, 1961	November 22, 1963	Died During First Term	Lyndon B. Johnson
Lyndon B. Johnson	Democrat	November 22, 1963	January 20, 1969	Completed Kennedy's Term, Served One Term	Office Vacant, Hubert H. Humphrey
Richard Nixon	Republican	January 20, 1969	August 9, 1974	Completed First Term, Resigned During Second Term	Spiro T. Agnew, Gerald Ford

PRESIDENT	PARTY	TOOK OFFICE	LEFT OFFICE	TERMS SERVED	VICE PRESIDENT
Gerald Ford	Republican	August 9, 1974	January 20, 1977	Completed Nixon's Second Term	Nelson A. Rockefeller
Jimmy Carter	Democrat	January 20, 1977	January 20, 1981	One	Walter Mondale
Ronald Reagan	Republican	January 20, 1981	January 20, 1989	Two	George H.W. Bush
George H.W. Bush	Republican	January 20, 1989	January 20, 1993	One	Dan Quayle
Bill Clinton	Democrat	January 20, 1993	January 20, 2001	Two	Al Gore
George W. Bush	Republican	January 20, 2001	January 20, 2009	Two	Dick Cheney
Barack Obama	Democrat	January 20, 2009			Joe Biden

"In the councils of government, we must guard against the acquisition of unwarranted influence, whether sought or unsought, by the military-industrial complex." Dwight D. Eisenhower

WRITE TO THE PRESIDENT

You may write to the president at:

The White House
1600 Pennsylvania Avenue NW
Washington, DC 20500

You may e-mail the president at:

comments@whitehouse.gov

GLOSSARY

allies - people, groups, or nations united for some special purpose. During World War II Great Britain, France, the United States, and the Soviet Union were called the Allies.

amendment - a change to a country's constitution.

chief of staff - the highest ranking officer in the U.S. Army or Air Force.

civil rights - the individual rights of a citizen, such as the right to vote or freedom of speech.

Constitution - the laws that govern the United States. Something relating to or following the laws of a constitution is constitutional.

demerit - a mark against a person for bad work or behavior.

Democrat - a member of the Democratic political party. Democrats believe in social change and strong government.

inaugurate (ih-NAW-gyuh-rayt) - to swear into a political office.

integrate - to end the separation of people by race and include everyone in society on an equal basis.

Korean War - from 1950 to 1953. A war between North and South Korea. The U.S. government sent troops to help South Korea.

memoirs (MEHM-wahrz) - a written account of a person's experiences.

missile - a weapon that is thrown or projected to hit a target.

National Guard - one of the voluntary military organizations of the U.S. Army and Air Force. Each state, each territory, and the District of Columbia has its own National Guard. Each unit is commanded by individual state governors and the president.

NATO - North Atlantic Treaty Organization. A group formed by the United States, Canada, and some European countries in 1949. It tries to create peace among its nations and protect them from common enemies.

Panama Canal - a human-made, narrow canal across Panama that connects the Atlantic and Pacific oceans. The Canal Zone was an area that began in the center of the canal and extended five miles (8 km) on each side.

polio - the common name for poliomyelitis, a disease that sometimes leaves people paralyzed. It usually affects children.

rebellious - resisting or refusing to obey authority.

Republican - a member of the Republican political party. Republicans are conservative and believe in small government.

riot - a sometimes violent disturbance caused by a large group of people.

running mate - a candidate running for a lower-rank position on an election ticket, especially the candidate for vice president.

satellite - a manufactured object that orbits Earth. It relays weather and scientific information back to Earth. It also sends television programs across Earth.

segregation (seh-grih-GAY-shuhn) - the separation of an individual or a group from a larger group, especially by race.

Supreme Court - the highest, most powerful court in the United States.

unconstitutional - something that goes against the laws of a constitution.

World War I - from 1914 to 1918, fought in Europe. Great Britain, France, Russia, the United States, and their allies were on one side. Germany, Austria-Hungary, and their allies were on the other side.

World War II - from 1939 to 1945, fought in Europe, Asia, and Africa. Great Britain, France, the United States, the Soviet Union, and their allies were on one side. Germany, Italy, Japan, and their allies were on the other side.

WEB SITES

To learn more about Dwight D. Eisenhower, visit ABDO Publishing Company on the World Wide Web at **www.abdopublishing.com**. Web sites about Dwight D. Eisenhower are featured on our Book Links page. These links are routinely monitored and updated to provide the most current information available.

INDEX